Easter in March

First published in 2016 by
Liberties Press
140 Terenure Road North | Terenure | Dublin 6W
T: +353 (1) 405 5701 | E: info@libertiespress.com | W: libertiespress.com

Trade enquiries to Gill & Macmillan Distribution
Hume Avenue | Park West | Dublin 12
T: +353 (1) 500 9534 | F: +353 (1) 500 9595 | E: sales@gillmacmillan.ie

Distributed in the United Kingdom by
Turnaround Publisher Services
Unit 3 | Olympia Trading Estate | Coburg Road | London N22 6TZ
T: +44 (0) 20 8829 3000 | E: orders@turnaround-uk.com

Distributed in the United States by
Casemate-IPM | 22841 Quicksilver Dr | Dulles, VA 20166
T: +1 (703) 661-1586 | F: +1 (703) 661-1547 | E: ipmmail@presswarehouse.com

ISBN: 978-1-910742-33-4
2 4 6 8 10 9 7 5 3 1

A CIP record for this title is available from the British Library.

Cover design by Liberties Press
Internal design by Liberties Press
Printed and bound in India by Thomson Press India Ltd.

Easter in March

Daragh Bradish

LIB
ERT
IES

For
Anne Fitzpatrick
Companion of this heart

Contents

Three

One must splice oneself, into some great circuit; but one must also insulate oneself, in order not to mischannel, not to use up, not to lose the current that one carries.

—Rainer Maria Rilke

Easter in March

It recurs; that day you stop and notice a window open in Rathgar
and on the sill a bowl of daffodils whose hollowed stalks bear up
their cups of dazzling yellow,

and in the dark interior the alcoves brighten as the light
of yet another room advances, another window opened south;
so you fill up with intimations of a life.

A woman's hands that held the vase beneath
⠀⠀⠀⠀the splashing waters of her tap;
that held the scissors, cut the stalks, and bore
⠀⠀⠀⠀her offerings to the house;
whose fingers tread the loops while levering the frame.

You lifted windows such as this one once, the weighted
⠀⠀⠀⠀iron on their ropes,
so young arms conquered all,
and leaning out beheld your springtime then,
⠀⠀⠀⠀as she has setting out her votive stall,

another March come round again to feed a heart's
⠀⠀⠀⠀old inclination.
An endlessness presents that reassures
though heaving forward, as something like spent love luffs by.

One

Broad Ditch

The canal is emptying of water:
prams and bicycles, cot-mattress springs,
metal holdings of another age,
stocked in sludge come slowly
to the surface – after lifetimes.

I stop to ponder Portobello dock
not *terra firma* this,
but plank that bears a foothold
you can pause on, take stock
of endless throwaways from.

This passage out, a broad ditch
running like torn flesh,
needs medication. Cauterised,
smells stick in nostrils
after the instinctive turnabout.

Swans once crossed reedy bank to bank
and will in time return to grace us,
nine hundred years from now,
that chosen hour of our redemption
after the healers decamp.

I imagine; waters splash back,
rushes rise to cover sharp-cut margins,
beautiful plume-headed pilgrims
come to reclaim our losses,
gathering like small children gather

such cast-offs they can make belief from.

Prelude

Before you dance again
      start with a collector's hand
to gather up from places
      you imagined empty
the put-asides once left
      on shelves awaiting rescue.

That day begin
      your promised comeback.
unwind.

Take time, that morning, to stop
      and read the weathervane
and with recovered ease
      then go outside again
to plant for spring,
      perhaps a dozen daffodils.

Primavera

This spring-born light invites reflection,
lifts latches, shutters pushed apart.

Optical illusions flourish in this still-not-summer.
Trees sprout umbrellas overnight,
weighted blossoms bent to earth.

Mary, Bridget and Persephone,
life-bringers, Botticelli-beauties,
flowers in arms, go barefoot on the grass.

A wane world altering
while human eye adjusts to sparkles,
we deck our indoor shrines, re-imaging first prayers.

First Memory: Portmarnock Strand

Wallflower wallflowers growing up so high
We're all pretty maidens who do not wish to die . . .

And this is the way of world!
Everything belongs here on
this crowded beach with family
about my grandmother
seated on a travelled chair.

Now out of nowhere comes
a chanting chain of weaving
wallflowers growing high above.
My dancing cousins who
do not wish especially to die.

I am unshelled coming to my feet,
sand spilling from my bucket,
spade in hand, I watch
as one girl is dropped and then another.

My grandmother drinking a last cup
nods at the waves and whispers,
'When everything comes together
there is still a hungry space'.

And this is the way of it then!
I with my empty bucket,
she in black-widow lace,
both of us awaiting the embrace
of expelled chosen flowers.

Homer's Daughter

I inherit nothing more than dismay

When you fall in my father's house
there shall be no man to avenge you.
    —*The Odyssey: Book 1*

Her father, a traveller, saw the world
and came home blinded.
Going out heroic, now he
was beggared for a friend.

A stranger in his home,
outside he named constellations,
Pegasus like treacle on his tongue,
sung password to oblivion.

At Christmas he told
his daughter about Homer
and put whiskey in the cat's milk.
She envisioned battles with

no standing room for mortals,
Gallipolis without her heroes,
falling like drunken cats
around the kitchen floor.

Radio Drifters

Our girl-aunt takes the morning up a beat,
circling the kitchen terracotta floor,
cream flour drifting from loose apron strings.

A shelf transistor moving
her every sure step forward,
receptor to *Some Kind of Wonderful*.

Small on margins, we stay static, doubtful
a fragile moment more, then stumbling
out of sequence into dance.

I could not, and never can explain
what happens next,
and happens every time again.

This unexpected lift of tenderness
in airborne song
awaking magic motion in our lives.

Sounds That Are Brightest

i.m. Florence O'Meara

Since you are gone it is your singing voice I hear.
Sounds of Maritana and the Kerry dances ringing clear
about the house on sun-bright mornings.

Sometimes a sad tune gave the cover-up to how you felt,
and with a pithy lyric on your lips you knelt,
and drew up more than faded flowers.

Once, you told me your dreams, painting with notation,
each flight from the heart, each emigration.
Only that music lasted through our lives.

This then is your returning gift to me. Once more,
today I rose from plucking weeds, and standing back, sore,
heard the sounds of past-loved summers sung.

Pathfinders

A window open to the summer night
allows the uninvited break-in,
street noise.

Holiday catcalls on the seaside breeze,
and easy amusement takers
break in song.

In our attic we cross a coral reef
and find the pathway to a
new adventure.

Safe on sand we turn our pockets out.
A twisted hook could one day
save a life.

We do not fear the unforeseen;
each page trailed by scouts
before us.

Tonight we start another book.
A girl is kidnapped on a
foggy moor.

I lie back fortified in iron bed,
the real-stuff soundtrack,
my imagination,

permitting time enough to risk
my neck in winter, going out
to rescue Lorna.

Gift Maker

He takes odd lengths of 2 by 2s

and from each foot of wood
he cuts six cubes.
Between his finger flesh
he rubs smooth every block,
          readies it.

Building pieces drop
to the workshop floor,
hand-crafted shapes
to sawdust sheeting. After tea-break,
         he unearths

the Stable, coats it
black. Blobs white
for snow on surface.
Finished; as a child might,
        he signs off with a dot.

When pale neighbours
cross our garden wall
and offer well-considered prayers,
lost for grown-up words,
       I show them

toy bricks I play with now,
a cave lit up with flashes;
holy spot-work; dust,
labour and delight
        before we blot it out.

The Tree of Idleness
in the Age of Discovery

When we had set the wilderness aside
and made great piles of tangled scourings,
the long-lost garden came to life again.
Traces of lawn and broken pathways
tumbled gateposts and a fallen shed,
fragmented leftovers of past summers,
became the Americas of childhood,
where only tall grown trees survived:
chestnut, pine and London plane.

One single standing monkey-puzzle,
sweeper branched with prehistoric
fingers, touched our bedroom window,
and on early summer mornings called us
to the promised land of our creation.
There among the outgrown branches
of a laurel grove, we built our hideaway.
A treehouse four foot off the ground
protection from the uninvited adult.

This was our place of morning rest,
afternoon retreat and evening layback.
Pilgrims shored in paradise,
we viewed a garden green with birth,
and feasted eyes of wanderlust.
This could be tamed in time, a continent
of exploration, though we remained
better cradled in the tentacles of trees,
the wayward offsprings of the earth.

Caveat

Somewhere   in the thicket there is wire,
a net line, measured out by hand,
which makes this boundary certain.
We are divided by growth of sixty years'
hedging which has sprung between us.

She unsettles   on the ground now
watching children play in trees
the ease of solitude entirely passes.
Her deckchair sinks in deeper every hour.
We are not what she expects as neighbours,
and disbelief seeps into paradise.
She lifts her cane to wag a warning:
we sway the leafy branches back and forth.

Disturbed   we will not find our way
to ground, clamp down, or take
the path from coppice to an open state.
Our side is wild and will remain tree-raised
a little longer, warned but still untamed.

Circuits

I used to jump off moving buses,
hold the bar and slightly sway
volta left and *basic bounce*,
a bit amazed, down to the pavement.
I almost learned to dance that way
        before I learned to dance.

First urged down by my mother's hand,
a natural back then –
I caught the undercurrent of the world.
Once waiting on a bus at night, my mother
hailed a cab, whose driver knew her
        from before the war.

Back home they chatted for an hour or more,
made strange connections over years.
He knew the house and shared
the laughter of a now dead pal
as they swung down our stair rail,
        tumbled into summer,

Then the TTs in the Isle of Man,
speeds achieved on mountain circuit,
Gooseneck, *Black Hut* and the *Verandah*.
then past the *Nook* to the finish line.
The friend he thought would be forever,
        the man my mother buried.

The driver sipped our whiskey but refused his fare.
He toasted other lives long vanished,
And through each story's twist I hung on tight,
gripped the newel post in our hall
until I felt my spine tingle, and I sprang
                out from the bottom step.

Two

Trespassers

The round moon up and gaping,
we cross the widest field I ever walked.
Fresh trenches run from side to side,
with tubers still in ridges, as yet no stalks,
and waiting on a warm spring swell
to heave their sprouting to the sky.

We have come from rough lands
on to cultivated ground.
My older gun-shouldered companions
disappointed. No game found
worth the kill. I follow at a distance,
step across each thrown-up mound,
and listen to their easy talk.

There is an old place
half a mile from here,
a fine house fallen into ruin,
almost a sanctuary.
That said, we end arriving at the door
open to whatever might come in.

The dank interior smells of death.
Windows with hanging spears of glass
like bare-fanged hunting hounds,
planked shutters pushed apart,
each room-corner festering a mass
of cobwebs. Pigeons everywhere

soon flushed to sudden flight.
An ear-split crack of gunshot
echoes through the house.
One bird splinters a frosted moon.

Brick Drops in Adolescence /
The Quality of Mercy

On Sunday we drop bricks on running rats,
this building site, a habitat of rodents.
My brother, the builder, stacks solutions,
man-made courses of a perfect wall.
Between drainpipes rats scurry for their lives.
A girl beguiles me, passing unaware
the spell she scatters with her yellow hair.
I drop more bricks and hurry to my tea.

Monday, and a teaching brother, the school boss,
sounds a warning bell.
You could grow up a hippy maybe, baby.
He always calls me baby, though this is unexpected
and about the length of hair.
Hair I am thinking these days can possess you,
hair belonging to another can possess you.
A golden anima, a turn of heart possess you.

Tuesday, role models required reading,
he wonders who my patron saints might be.
Francis of Assisi I now throw back.
Your brother I admire your brother,
if I was starting life I'd go into the building,
lots of money coming out of bricks,
                              bricks have uses.
Didn't Francis build a church with bricks?

That was with heaps of moss-wrapped stones, drop-outs,
imperfections.

A poet, he laughs and walks, no subtle touch about him.
O baby, surely you must be for the birds.

Banshee Calling

Perhaps it was that night she sang *Suzanne*
that our age of Aran sweaters ended.
Perched on the blades of Leonard Cohen's song,
she launched her warning note, suspended
from family, church and civilisation,
or whatever we were chanting on the night
good grace fell victim to her winged citation.
Like birds decamping from the emerald shore,
on one more flight to an encroaching desert,
she hooked our knitted dinosaur
and made with it, claw interlocking hand,
off to her relocated houseboat
where she had planned some floating menu
of sacred scrapings that were both old and new.

Grace Notes in December

Together every now and then
you and snow-wet streets
would be returned a pair
of sisters in a fairy window,
whose frost-framed mirror
beamed with tiny coloured treats.

The city too would open wide
long thin inviting arms
and by and by we'd slide
upon a drunk and drowsy smile
that said we had no need
of lists or calendar-decked charms.

Streets and shops, stars at night,
churches scenting waxy
and every now and then,
the casual acquaintance
of a stray prayer waiting
on the next bus home, or taxi.

Hemerocallis

I was the fool who never spoke,
for speaking I could tell her merely
that I remembered how her green kerchief
was used to demonstrate a Chevreul theory.
Or that I saw her hesitate quite briefly
in Grafton Street, one morning early.

I was the fool who could not speak,
when captured in enchanted haze,
we drank of Monet or the art of Flanders,
on Friday afternoons in academic days,
with one companion more beautiful
than tongue-tied poetry could praise.

I was the fool who would not speak,
until a lily in a bed of weeds
returned the promise of another year.
A green kerchief that served its needs.
Beauty demands blood, while silence,
breaking no hearts, nevertheless bleeds.

Swimming in the Aquarium

Their first summer, she wished him plant a hedge.
Cyprus leylandii, the nurseryman suggested.
They grow up fast. Get bushy ones,
dig deep, and early on, be sure you water well.

She lay back hopeful as her lover went to work.
Following good counsel he planted forty trees
in perfect rows each side a lush green lawn,
then after dark, guilt-free, broke the hosepipe ban.

Early September they went island-hopping
carelessly through Greece, mad and infatuated
they made best plans by day, nightly they made love.
Back home a neighbour kept their saplings wet.

One day she took the dare and swam naked in the sea.
Finding it pulsate with life, she skipped back out.
Holding her beach towel he came to meet her.
Child-bearing hips, his comment – their shared laughter.

The wall of trees grew fast, reaching a desired height.
Screening for everything was what she'd asked for.
Though possible to sunbathe now, in privacy,
she longs for shoals of swarming fish.

Love Child

In the mother's body we know the universe.
In birth we forget it.
                              —Jewish proverb

Whichever way it aims, it takes you to the centre
of your space.
You have crossed the threshold and the manual
is useless now,
exactitude of meaning, pointless in face
of Titian's painting Sacred and Profane Love.

Sketching in colours from the start, the artist
in his time
returned to caress this canvas child,
his art
blending tones and adding line to line,
composed the final tincture with his fingers.

The invented title will not process further,
so wait
while you unearth the possibility of
wording.
Arms and feet are bound by fate,
some elsewhere you remember folded wings,

dim-sighted Titian making means by touch.

Building Venice

And had I known I was an island-maker
I'd have chosen well each stone,
buffing smooth the surface in my hand
before I let it drop coldly to the water,
and listened with a seasoned ear
to note the plop and ripples as it sank.
And so with our fresh dreams,
could we be watchful while they drift
to base, then rise up gleaming,
layer on sunken layer, to form,
a pellicle of sun-warmed sea,
where they compose, lap and gurgle,
waiting to be land or life imagined.
Vivaldi on a seashell surfing to the shore.

Morning Radio

In half-light morning
I catch a song I used to know
but had let slip.

She sings it as a child would,
snatching rhymes
from gathered wild things.

Her uncupped palms
send butterflies
across the waking planet

And music circulates
along the city laneways
to a garden gate.

Bolted doors unlock,
silent fears put aside
like winter clothing.

Only then
day breaks
beyond the expected news-line.

A Ghost at Noon

Today's heat triggers memory. Lunchtime
sunshine in the city so kissable that anything might happen.
A man might walk the surface of another moon.

Escaping offices, lovers seek hideaways,
canal-side refuge giving shelter for their hour.
I stop the car, want to cause upheaval,
      flip a switch and lift off out of time.

It happens. The summer of sixty-nine comes towards me
      tossing back her hair.
This teenage fighter with the free flag *Lunacy*
takes form and rises from a noon-hot haze;

a ghost girl made visible until a flash of amber
sends me back to base, so consciously
I swallow air and splash-land somewhere in the Pacific Ocean.

Chikuni

for Dónall O'Murchú

The swimming pool you built in Africa
has turned into a fish-pond.
Soon you will have to start from silt,
pour concrete into old foundations,
watch while it settles.

Dig deeper and draw breath.
A stone-breaker sits beneath the mango tree,
his piecework spread like scattered seed.
The water tower on stilts,
a question mark on cloudless blue.

As in the beginning, everything in play,
lizards, snakes, fisher birds await the starter.

Remember
going forward on hot sands
scaling snow-encrusted mountains,
trusting man-weight on frozen waters,
coming to the land-ledge of security.

Hovering a day there counting obstacles,
you saw Skellig crowned with hungry birds,
its stone huts clotted on the rock-face,
a steeple against cloudy grey,
then went down to Chikuni, dug another hole.

From Mullaghmore

That summit opened us
as morning eyes make
things familiar fresh.

We scanned
our landscapes,
vast and handleless,

The giant's playground
all about us,
gauged our lives.

Sun on waters,
Shadow-mottled fields,
unembraceable, immense.

So we descended,
took the trail
of seeded touchstones,

crossed table rock,
split *scailp*s filled
with marginals;

sneezewort, selfheal,
grass of Parnassus.
Small recognitions,

windswept things
that brought us through
our length of summers.

Stranger

i.m. John O'Donohue

At the bottom of the mountain turn,
and take the green route through the thicket,
between lace walls, each stone
weighted on its neighbour's back.
Chinks filter the prevailing winds.
Be mindful always of each sound.
A little distance on, you will locate
the entrance, if you can,
by a miracle too small to throw you.
Notice, the gate of fine-woven saplings
and crafted sign, a riddle by the hand of man.
A short walk and you reach the source.
Spittle rising from the ground,
a cup left hanging from a branch.

Pilgrim Siftings at Liscannor

I came upon a child of God
Walking along the road
                    —Joni Mitchell

We have come full circuit on the strand.
Woodstock assembled at a west Clare bay.
Neighbours with garlands, gathering to pray,
the words made fresh for us today,
this moment in this sacred land,
this place behind the desert where we stand.

Above our heads the ruined church-walls hold
bones of ancestors sleeping on the cliff,
abstractions and intangibles caught in sieve,
we in the here and now dreaming an alternative
walk with handheld flowers to fold,
into returning seas, the sins we never told.

Three

Small Lives

Boy in a Box, Reading

Nothing settles
in this market turmoil

but the boy
within four sides of crating

who takes a book
and folds back covers

while waiting
on his mother to complete

morning orders
at each dealer's stall.

Girl at the Holy Well

Her tribe bent
forward

to the ancient source,
she is looking

at short distance,
wonders in the sharpened lens.

Will she need
father's reading specks

or mother's
Sunday headscarf.

Sacrament

for Anne

We have moved to a new location,
the possibility that holiness seeks no exceptions.
Here is the photograph.
You on a backless bench beside a dock,
the Slovene town of Bled beneath its rock,
the third day of our marriage.

Bearing what is yet unframed or seen,
a swan arises from that space between
you by the lake, and me with the camera.
Wide wingspan marks its gateway into flight,
and morning, enchanting common sight,
turns sacred almost everything.

The Boy in the Boat

for Anne

That day, I took you on the water,
you worried I might drown,
as if the fact I couldn't swim was new.
As if I didn't know the danger then.
The lift and fall, the lap and pull
of travelling blind into the middle lake,
oars slicing the obstacle; black liquid,
still and unimaginably deep.

I heard your voice, which does not carry,
tell me *please turn round the boat*.
Shoreline sliding beyond your shoulders
further from the crowded dock. I let it float
a little while on calm, then with a single pull,
began to circle and draw back.

A Little Bit Funny

When they handed you the key
To Elton John's piano,
you expressed your unexpected honour.

Thank you thank you thank you,
you told the academy of desire,
thank you, endlessly translated from the Irish.

Your audience unleashed applause.
Wicked plants are plentiful, you quoted,
and one brought death to Lincoln's mother.

Going forward you wished to walk on walls,
avoid the garden after dinner
and do creative writing on the roof.

Now Fly Me to the Moon

for Robert

A set-down area for passengers with flights to catch.
I drop your luggage, leave the engine purr.
Just as we planned it, your departure is as effortless
    as a door closing.
I drive off to maintain composure; the past in cold
    storage,
your room without furniture.

When you were two – *an image of your father* –
I charmed you with a space voyage to the moon,
your treasures carried in a cardboard rocket.
A cake, a toy, a grip of kitchen gems we loved to dine on.
The small nest-eggs of living then, were size enough
    to pocket.

At lift-off you abandoned ship, ran to your mother's
    arms,
one tiny slip from courage.
What scared you on the moon-face that time, scares
    me now.
You left me in my spacebox cut adrift,
our trip in capsule put on hold.

The future softly touching down,
a blue globe hung above us;
your child-size fingers pointing up,
and plastic cup, fork and knife spread out with care
upon a lunar sea of shared tranquillity.

We Seek Directions

Our third visit and the journey north
splinters history like an axe.

Ancient farms and factories,
old battlefields and hillside vineries,
the abbey squatting on its mountain,
each windowframe, small fraction
of the one hour's travel time
from Naples by express track.

Passing shots slow only
for our arrival back at station point.

'Eternal city of the Popes'
you murmur; I concur.

We shoulder bags across the platform
and work a passage to the streets
where brightly coloured Vespas buzz
through anxious saints and pilgrims.

Still puzzled by the barbarians,
we seek directions to the Coliseum.

Postcard from Rome

This day's matins:
rain falling in the palazzo gardens;
we cross the walling and watch the downfall
dribble to its close.

Now seated.
Over biscuits and coffee
we select our postcard,
and code it for assured delivery.

Another age,
I mad-dashed from the square,
caught breath on the Janiculum
and pegged each prayer upon an antique pine.

Lunchtime,
near the Coliseum,
our order scribbled on his docket,
the waiter looks sideways to the street.

Urbi et Orbi.
Our postcard from Rome,
A little rain today allows us
time to write you.

Palm Sunday

There were, in his mind, many other shapes – of people and
places, of philosophies and poems.
          —Charles Williams, *The Figure of Beatrice*

All day along the city streets
among the pilgrims and the pressing throng
I saw them walk with Passion sprays
like mistletoe hung loosely by their untouched sides,
lovers wrapped in one another's gaze,
naked in the abandonment of creed
though dressed enough to thrill these human eyes,
creators of the chic, statement-makers
of youth and beauty feeding the desire
to be at once admired. And yet the whittled branches
of the old beliefs in something still in wait for us
beyond this present carriage, the sublime.

As I came early from the narrow way
that opened on the piazza, the chiaroscuro
of the grand basilica cast before me
like a peddler's throw, which, scattered with enticements,
cloaks the ground, I caught the now enchantment
of a Roman spring; the love of Earth
and Heaven all at one with man.
But I had known before, the grave inspector's stalk,
trappings of delight scooped up in seconds.
pavements left tonsured and polite, the traders muffled
and in the shades, white eyes as give-aways
of human life in fear of judgment.

Cantor-like, the bells cried out
across the terracotta sprawl of rooftops
spread below us from the Spanish Steps,
the route by which we made our staged decent
to where the youthful poet fretted out his call.
The man who named truth Beauty, wrenched.
Was it enough to know, I wondered,
this much and nothing more. Gregorian,
the chant had swelled our hearts
when the procession passed us through the door
of Santa Maria Maggiore that morning.
We inhaled centuries of smoke.

That we might be found beautiful
and not be damned, had failed my comprehension
until I gleaned the young of Rome
embedded in delight, arm held but free of doubt.
I saw them linger by the river among the stalls
below the Castel Sant'Angelo, Pilate's question
on my whetted lips and Keats' reply.
Then looking up with keened perception
I caught Bernini's angels looking down;
swooning, creatures in ecstasy, bearing
mighty feathered wings, and fixed to the bridge-rail,
clasping the holy instruments of torture.

Olivia

Poised on parapet above
the deep arena she displays
her morning beauty to the crowd.

Breath held, her figure
draws attentions to its shape,
and lens-clutching seekers
take the bait.

They would, if etiquette allowed,
begin to shower their pointed shots.

But she is all for him,
the chosen lover,
at least until he posts
her taken-picture on the Net.

Olivia observed alive in Rome,
shines out her peers;
who come through ancient
vomitorium

to marvel this achievement,
engineered perfection;
brick bone striped of marble glazing,
Coliseum.

Olivia,
a short-lived smile,
which fronts the dark
round abyss of desire, a pit

of dungeons panting
to the blistering sun.
But only mortal visitors persist,
intent upon the object gaze;

that left hand resting
on a curve of hip-bone,
and right hand thrusting forward,
twisted wrist,

that one small opposable thumb,
caught pointing to her feet,
his cell-phone held
before her like a blade.

Turnabout in the Age of Recovery

I have come tonight to that place I called home.
The curve of railings caved in the narrow road,
tangled weave replaced with tubular steel,
now galvanised and fashioned for convenience.

I used to paint old crumbling bars for days,
working my brushes through scrolls and trellises,
flat-hammered ivy leaves, webs of rust,
till blisters burst in protest on young palms.

I have come without arrangement to this place,
finding myself in the vicinity of want,
to call my past and fond entanglements to shine,
recast our bonded seams of love.

The garden has grown smaller now;
grass given up to hard-core, driveway boxed
into a safe containment, windows shuttered
after working hours, the building set aside.

Street-lights are bedded in the trees
about this closed-off space; shadows flicker;
quaking shapes afford me no security.
I grew in wonder once but there is nothing

keeps me still, only cold knowledge
of no shunting place along the road.
Old Hand, I grip the steering hold;
Helmsman, score each callus on my skin.

Storm Beach

Bray, County Wicklow, 2014

January, the sea heaved lunging at the strand,
demanding restoration of the beach, before the work of man
shaped a resort, with all desired amenities.
Back to unpredictability of place,
steep embankment of sand and stones and thrown-up real surprise,
before a promenade was levelled out and laid
between the river mouth and headland jutting into shallows.

Returning with the gaze of one who travels back to walk the shore,
I try imagining the ancient line.
An open free place, a migratory world
forever changing with each season's flow,
that took a Roman shipwreck in its stride and swooped up whole.
Those who did not survive, the sailors buried in the dunes,
with coin in mouth to pay whatever fare might fall.

As children taught in this ocean-harried town, we fed
        the self-same gods,
chanced slot machines in an Arcadia indifferent to our cares.
Not always in expectation of some lucky strike
answering our prayers, we learnt
the knack of looking both ways at the surge.

Missing

The dispatch warns of snow on higher ground.
Already it is falling as we reel the row-boat back,
silent men retiring to the shed.

This called-for hush is broken by the boy
who wonders how them paddlesticks were lost.
The hull hauled into resting place,
the door slams over.

Surely words are called for, surely prayers.
The small boy thinks we ought go fetch them oars,
start trawling sea-spaghetti on the shore.
But it is dark now

and, blinded by cold speckles from a frozen sky
we wrap our faces with coarse woollen scarves,
hand-knitted vestments,
murmer and push on.

Soundings

Crossing over, you almost fail to notice
how iron arches from each quay,
its old frame set belly-up above the river.

Easing weight, the bridge
bears all its passengers with grace,
so walking over water equals flight.

Natural dancer, you sidestep
the incumbent on the halfpenny gallows,
only slip a beat,

the void between one long note
sounding and another groan
of bolted metal holding tight.

Uncertain/Macreehy's Bed, Liscannor Bay

for Denis Crosbie

A' Raibh Tú ag an gCarraig
No an bhfaca fein mo ghrá?

The singer searches our response
here at the margins of the bay.
Her tempered voice is lilting
soft as distant days,
her every pause of breath considered.

I would like to tell her yes,
I was here and saw your loved one,
and *oh yes, he was still*
asking after you,
but truth is I have no answer for her.

On each return,
wafted from the strand,
the rawness of this places confronts me,
exposing little crabs
that scamper rock to rock and hide.

I join with wavers, souls
who seek the salt-encrusted stone.
The sea-wash levelling
these human punctures; our imprints
spill out with water and dissolve.

Credo

Sunday-morning ebb tide
    we could walk the bay
almost without end,
    the flat sands rising
to a pearl-white sky.

Now pocket pools invite
    curious small pilgrims,
whose booted feet
    splash hip-high rains
on their indulgent father.

One man grips a sky-kite,
    floats from the ground,
struggles though ordained
    to fall,
the gull-cries circling his head.

We sit still with our books,
    between the pages glance
at passing strangers,
    dogs on long leashes,
their keepers elsewhere.

Spangles of broken light
    dust open palms.
Your fingers, tracing words
    and folded bookends,
sense miracles, tidings.

The far-out sea crawls back,
     our strandline narrows.
I do not know if I believe it,
     as someone said they saw us,
Sunday, holding hands.

Night Music

at Dun Laoghaire harbour

Tonight within the harbour walls
small craft seem almost motionless.

Masts vertical like half-hammered nails
against the glow or afterglow of sun.
Distance playing her old tricks on us.

Reefed naked for the night, we think
these boats are going nowhere,
lazing on settled sea, anchored down

and still. Chimes from every stopping place
pass mouth to mouth a faint determination
to explore, move in formation.

Some other music comes and goes.
The banjo man is peppering his strings;
familiar reels skip freely from his fingers.

The drop-box open for our change,
he sets his pitch before us, so we move,
always imagining a distance from the end.

Notes

'Sounds That Are Brightest'
Scenes That Are Brightest from William Wallace's 'Maritana'

'Hemerocallis'
Day lily, each flower lasting only one day. Hemeracallis – new Latin. From the Greek , *hemera* (day) and *kallos* (beauty).

'Chikuni'
The Chikuni mission is in the southern province of Zambia.

Storm Beach
In 1835 workmen digging foundations in the dunes near Bray Head came upon a Roman burial with several human bodies. On exposure to the air the bones crumbled, only coins and teeth remaining intact.

Uncertain / Macreehy's Bed, Liscannor Bay
A' Raibh Tu ag an gCarraig, No an bhfaca fein mo ghra? Were you at the rock, Did you see my loved one?

Acknowledgments

The author is grateful to the editors of the following journals, where some of the poems in this collection first appeared:

Revival Literary Journal: 'Homer's Daughter', 'Building Venice'

Crannog: 'Stranger', 'Hemerocallis'

The Moth: 'First Memories', 'Portmarnock Strand'

Equinox: 'Prelude'

Orbis International Literary Journal: 'Morning Radio', 'The Boy in the Boat', 'Primavera', 'Radio Drifters'

Boyne Berries: 'Pathfinders'

Poetry Salzburg Review: 'Night Music', 'Soundings', 'Circuits'

★

I would like express my thanks to the following poets for their support, advice and encouragement:

Una Ni Cheallaigh

And Q   Tom Conaty

           Seamus Cashman

           Paul Bregazzi

Also, my thanks to the editor and staff at Liberty Press.